Decomprose

Haiku, short poems & thoughts

By John Duran

*I want to thank my wife Ellen, who encouraged me to write
a haiku every day for a year.*

*And Richard Alpert, aka Ram Dass, who told me he thought;
'your haikus would make good toilet reading'.*

—JD

Decomprose

Haiku, short poems & thoughts

By John Duran

My daily haiku,
Is just to say something true,
And share it with you.

–John Duran

Table of Contents

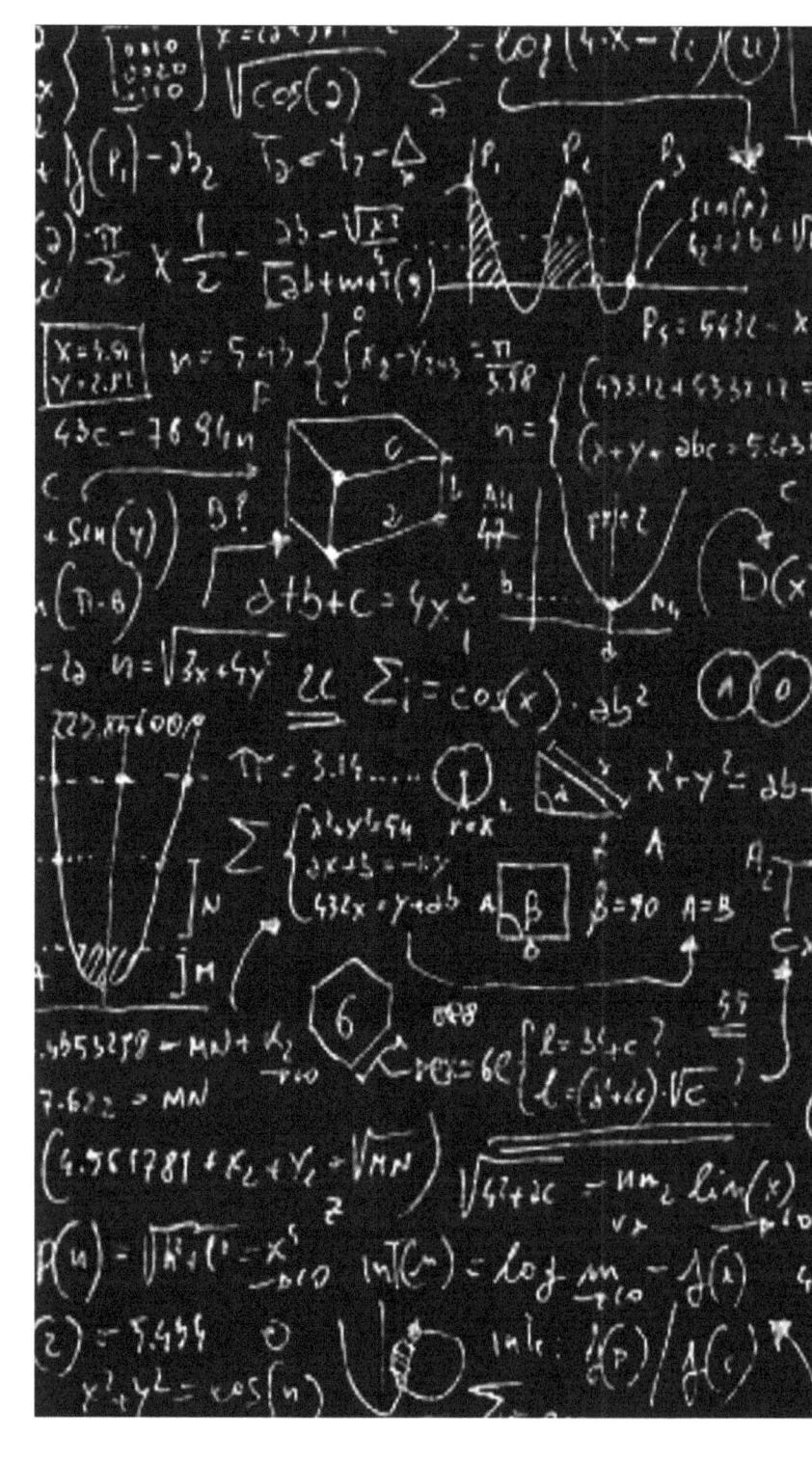

About Haiku

Haiku is a very short form of Japanese poetry typically characterised by three qualities:

> The essence of haiku is "cutting" (kiru). This is often represented by the juxtaposition of two images or ideas and a kireji ("cutting word") between them, a kind of verbal punctuation mark which signals the moment of separation and colors the manner in which the juxtaposed elements are related.
>
> Traditional haiku consist of three phrases of 5, 7 and 5 on respectively. Any one of the three phrases may end with the kireji. Haiku are often stated to have 17 syllables.
>
> A kigo (seasonal reference), usually drawn from a saijiki, an extensive but defined list of such words. The majority of kigo, but not all, are drawn from the natural world.

Modern Japanese gendai haiku are increasingly unlikely to follow the tradition of 17 on or to take nature as their subject, but the use of juxtaposition continues to be honoured in both traditional haiku and gendai.

—From Wikipedia

My poetry is derived from the haiku tradition but departs from it in many ways—primarily by rhyming. Although I stick to three-lines, I don't always follow the 5-7-5 format. Often my poems can be read with just the first and third lines, creating a separate thought within a poem.

Nature

First light never waits,
Morning never hesitates,
Beauty radiates.

Our lives are like trees,
Evolve like the birds and the bees,
Dissolve like the leaves.

Breath of coastal breeze,
Misty valley full of trees,
Salt spray makes me sneeze.

Particles and waves,
Reality's just a phase,
How universe plays.

Like welcoming smile,
Rainbows only last awhile,
Wow, life's sure got style.

All life is toil,
Even flowers lean toward the light
To break through soil.

Heart beats itself to death,
Ocean ebbs and flows,
Universe takes breath.

River in the skies,
Mesmerize and cries,
Rainbows fill my eyes.

Winters' blustery bite,
Snow glistens in frozen night,
Reflecting moonlight.

Burnt umber chilled trees,
Nature brings us to our knees,
Leaf drifts in the breeze.

Full moon floats on lake,
From our slumber we awake,
And melt like snowflake.

Moonlight fills my eyes,
Moaning oak trees frame the skies,
Mornings will surprise.

Sun sets in slow motion,
Silence roars like an ocean,
My heart soars in devotion.

Dancing in the breeze,
Look up and fall to my knees,
Ancient redwood trees.

Herons swoop and fly,
Popcorn clouds dissolve in sky,
Sunset tears in my eyes.

Watercolor skies,
Full moon on the rise,
Stars' dust in my eyes.

Foggy nights' surprise,
Crickets create a disguise,
Owls with full moon eyes.

Peach blossoms explode
As infinite unfolds
Nature's seeds are sowed

Wise man always knows
Nature flows where nature goes and
Which way the wind blows.

Springtime's wild pursuit,
Chestnut roots shoot from fall's fruit,
Nature's got new suit.

Orange blossom romance,
In Ojai the trees dance,
Intoxicating fragrance.

Spring comes like new friend,
Hawks hide in clouds and swoop in,
Carpets of lupine.

Winter's patchwork fleece,
Another season's release,
Wildflowers wave in peace.

Dawn breaks horizon,
Full moon skies put disguise on,
Sun wakes up rising.

Damp as winter's coat,
Songbirds clear their throats,
Sounds like velvet notes.

Uncommon Sense

My dad always said:
Better to have common sense
Than dollars and cents.

Fate is whimsical,
Chance can be fickle,
Time melts like a popsicle.

Be happy not sadder,
Crazy as the Mad Hatter,
Time and space don't matter.

Even angels wail,
Our pain doesn't mean we failed,
Winds will always fill our sails!

There's no thing to know,
It's all about trusting the flow,
So relax and let go!

You're happy or sad,
You're disappointed or glad,
Who's to say what's really bad?

Mind's on stay cation,
Travel's such a temptation,
Freedom's my own creation.

Your tickets been bought,
So give it all that you got!
You're all in or not?

No more preparation,
The train has left the station,
Time for destination.

Don't give up power,
Life can be sweet or sour,
Fresh as spring flower.

Our thoughts and our fears,
Are like clouds full of tears,
That eventually clears.

Each day of life is a test,
Hold on to the best,
Let go of the rest.

Big fish small pond,
Small fish big pond,
Just depends which side you're on!

Saturdays are great,
Stay in bed till late.
It's Mondays we hate!

Educate, don't medicate.
Illuminate, don't dominate.
Cast your fate, don't sit and wait.

An ounce of inspiration,
Pound of perspiration,
Ton of preparation.

Hungry for a feast?
If you want the pain to cease,
Tame your inner beast.

There's nowhere to hide,
Bright lights mask our darker side,
Camouflaged by pride.

Know me as your cause,
Know me through your flaws,
Know me through your moment's pause.

Live in gratitude.
It's more than a platitude,
It's your attitude.

First to come is first to go,
And the last don't last so long,
So learn to go with the flow.

To love and be clear,
Resolutions for New Year,
To live without fear.

It is what it is,
So don't dismiss or resist,
Or you'll miss it.

Faith hopes for the best,
Trust knows we're all blessed,
Love feathers the nest.

Imagine your dreams,
Beyond anything you've seen,
Wake up in between.

All moments in time,
Strung like laundry on the line,
Just states in our mind.

Every moment's forever,
Always grateful for whatever,
Every day's my best day ever.

Our failure or fame
Goes by many names.
Only thing constant is change.

Better you're a giver.
You get what you deliver.
Can't fight the river.

Vanity's a waste,
No sense saving face,
Humility is grace.

Who cares if you're first?
Caught in hubris,
It's an endless universe.

Humility is
A sign of greatness,
Of grace's loving patience.

We make such a fuss.
Who's got it better than us?
When is there enough?

Ever stop to think,
When you're feeling out of sync,
You're the missing link.

Greed feeds hungry beast,
Everyone comes to the feast,
When will madness cease?

Our futures evolve
As our ignorance dissolves,
Through strength and resolve.

Conceive positively,
Perceive universally,
Receive gracefully.

What colors your day?
So many shades of gray,
It's your brush, painting away.

Thunder rolling like a train,
Lightning strikes my brain,
Then the rainbows came.

All of creation,
Waits in anticipation,
For moment's inspiration.

Life's road unravels
So many paths to travel,
Some smooth, some gravel.

We are all Art-ists,
Experience is our color,
Life is our canvas.

Cosmic Dust

We seek purity,
Strive for security,
Slip into obscurity.

DNA can suck!
Genetics or just dumb luck,
Gandhi or Donald Duck?

Now can be twisted,
Blink and you missed it,
Eternity's an instant.

Though our minds insist
Time doesn't exist,
It's the moment we resist!

We struggle and fight
To do what is right.
Fruit falls from the tree when ripe.

Empathy not sympathy,
Understanding not demanding,
Compassion not reaction.

Scared to death of life,
Scared of life to death,
Every moment's all that's left!

Go to any length?
Success robs us of our strength.
Failure is a Saint!

Vanity's silly,
We all have the ability,
Greatness lies in humility.

Time is a river,
And every drop runs to sea,
The current is me.

The Future is Now,
Each moment is Now,
It's never not Now!

We look without seeing,
To escape without leaving,
From the selves we are being.

Now is forever,
Mind is too clever,
Time is past, future and never!

Always here and now,
Wherever you go, EGOs,
Nowhere else to go!

No things ever lost,
No things ever gained,
No things ever the same.

To hide our insecurities,
We mask vulnerabilities,
Behind hostilities.

Blessed to be born,
No choice where, when or the form,
Rejoice and perform.

We're too slow to budge,
Self-righteously hold a grudge,
And too quick to judge.

Middle of the night,
Darkest shadow of the light,
A moment's insight.

What makes us lucky?
Why not a junkie?
Who is the hundredth monkey?

Locked in our beliefs,
Limited by what we see,
Though we hold the keys.

Moments pass your eyes,
Wind chimes mesmerize,
Life's more than we realize.

Our reason admonishes,
Our wisdom astonishes,
Ocean polishes.

Intelligent emotions,
Transcend ebb and flow motions.
Intuitive notions.

What everyone knows,
and What history clearly shows,
We all DECOMPROSE!

Love, Family & Friendship

Hearts broken open,
When no one feels like coping,
Love's always hoping.

Soul loves through our eyes,
Heart loves through our smiles,
Our spirt loves to surprise.

Baby cries in bed,
Old man forgets what he said,
Both need to be fed.

Glad when I come home,
Never on the phone,
Always loves a bone!

Candle in the wind,
Flame traces where we have been,
Love glows from within.

Love's a baby's cry,
Love's the moment we die,
Love's spirit that flies.

Child clings to mother,
With the strength of a lover,
A bond like no other.

Sunrise is dawning,
The ghost of darkness is gone,
Even the cats yawning.

Everyone's got a part,
Now is a good time to start,
Love's an open heart.

Love is: A baby babbling,
A dying man rattling,
A moment unraveling.

We all have the power,
To be fearless or cower,
Love is a flower.

Love is all we need,
Love is the hunger we feed,
Love is the seed we conceive.

All you need is Love,
John Lennon said it the best,
Each moment's the test.

Schoolyard laughter shrieks,
Ivy walls where wisdom seeks,
Whisper of love speaks.

In a spiritual drought,
Lost in fear and doubt?
Without love, there's no way out.

Moon glows through light mist,
Springs as fresh as your first kiss,
Some things can't be missed.

Families love and nourish,
Experience strength and courage,
Help us grow and flourish.

Friends will inspire,
Ignite our inner fire,
Teach us to reach higher.

Goods friends mingling,
As clam chowder's simmering,
Oceans glimmering.

Spirituality & Religion

Our death is rebirth,
As sure as the sky and earth,
Are stardust and surf.

Just a drop in the ocean,
Where'd we get notion,
We're separate motion?

Wisdom beyond thought,
Go where no reason is sought,
Psychic astronaut.

We can't stop the rust,
But there's one thing we can trust,
We are all star's dust.

You know what he wants,
To be everywhere at once,
And nowhere at all.

No need to ever fear it,
Silence can hear it,
Everywhere spirit.

Don't be a hater,
Souls much greater,
Light loves Darth Vader.

Whose God would dream this,
So filled with meanness,
Religious extremist!

Murder in the name of Gods,
Barren as blood-soaked sod,
Righteousness is a facade!

Souls are like stars in the night,
Even when out of our sight,
Never stop shining their light.

Is haiku a koan?
Can truth be known?
Are our souls' seeds sown?

History of Papal,
Magnificent Sistine Chapel,
Don't eat that apple!

Will we ever see,
I am you and you are me,
We're come-unity.

Energy changes form,
Like costumes we've worn,
Everything dies to be reborn.

War makes me vomit,
Buddha, Christ and Mohammed,
Never would bomb it!

I'm not afraid of death.
Eternal life, I have no doubt.
It's dying I'm not crazy about.

Fear is the prison,
Perception is our prism,
Faith's spirit risen.

Though death makes us cry,
Birth opens our eyes,
Life's energy never dies!

Life is divine by design,
Accident in time,
Or your state of mind?

The tide ebbs and flows,
Universal heart beat knows,
Where the stardust goes.

We peddle and coast,
Between Hell's heavenly hosts,
No escape from hungry ghosts.

When our heart's aching,
The dawn is breaking,
Spirit's awakening.

Circles only bend,
Tide always comes in again,
Life will never end!

Fear without showing,
Faith without knowing,
Grace is death's face glowing.

Our spiritual dross,
Born of the fear of our loss,
Is just our soul's floss.

Soul is ever wise,
Sees through death's clever disguise,
Spirit never dies!

Search Hell for any light,
Doesn't end the spiritual blight,
Church bells ring all night!

History & Politics

History calls them greedy,
Indian lands roamed freely,
White man calls them treaties!

The big game hunters,
Who rape and plunder,
Beware of Karmic thunder!

Promises broken,
Genocide spoken,
Here's your land token,
You've got to be jokin'.

Distraught father cries,
Couldn't control pain inside,
Shaken baby dies.

Damp as winter's coat,
It's no wonder they lose hope.
How the homeless cope?

Gun lovers debate
Childrens deadly fate,
While Congress masturbates!

News at eleven
Child nine shot to heaven,
AK-47!

Out of no-thing takes order,
Out of some-thing comes borders,
Doubt of every-thing makes hoarders.

Human souls were tossed,
Seeds of generations lost,
Horrors of Holocaust.

The stock market roars,
While middle class sweeps the floors,
Corporate profit soars.

Banks too big to fail,
You'd think they're the Holy Grail,
Wizard behind veil.

Forget how it's always been,
Divided by Us and Them,
Too high a price to win.

Evil to the core,
What in Gods' name is it for?
Middle Eastern war.

Young men, old nation,
The ultimate sacrifice,
Abomination!

Pastimes
Travel and Sports

Balmy summer daze,
Always remember the ways,
Lose ourselves in play.

Life is a journey.
Why do we always hurry?
No need to worry.

With some it's a game,
With some it's a pain,
We drag our own ball and chain.

Life is just a game,
We're drawn to failure or fame,
Like a moth to flame!

Joy's a little boy,
Whose spirit can't be destroyed.
Life's his little toy!

Wild game hunted lame,
Once great herds, now none remain,
Trophys hang in shame.

Amsterdam, City of Bikes,
Canals full of golden lights,
What a magical sight.

Mediterranean sand,
Looks like Disneyland,
I'm a Cinque Terra fan!

In China there's a Great Wall,
Twenty million had to fall,
It's a landmark now!

Time is hard to believe,
A concept we conceive.
How do we arrive before we leave?

Farmers buy their ox,
Shanghai buys their stocks,
China's a paradox.

Tired of the raining,
Mired and complaining,
I'm going to spring training.

Baseball's a great game,
Fail seven out of ten times,
You're in Hall of Fame!

Our national game,
Played by little boy names,
Destined for the Hall of Fame.

www.ingramcontent.com/pod-product-compliance
Lightning Source LLC
Chambersburg PA
CBHW051254120626
46547CB00014B/1945

*9 7 9 8 2 1 8 5 8 5 5 7 0 *